Anjali the Brave
All About Vaccines

by Dr. Adjoa Smalls-Mantey & Dr. Maria Abraham
Illustrations by Paul Buşte

While we realize that masks should be worn in a variety of real-world
settings, they are not included in several illustrations to allow children to
see facial expressions and help them identify with the characters.
We recommend wearing masks in accordance with public health
guidance.

INDIES UNITED PUBLISHING HOUSE, LLC

ISBN: 978-1-64456-407-3 (Hardcover)
ISBN 978-1-64456-410-3 (EPUB)
ISBN: 978-1-64456-408-0 (Paperback)

Library of Congress Number: 2021950526

First Edition

INDIES UNITED PUBLISHING HOUSE, LLC
P.O. BOX 3071
QUINCY, IL 62305-3071

www.indiesunited.net

In memory of those lost to infectious diseases, and in honor of the scientists who worked to keep us safe.
-Adjoa-

For all my boys: Mogan, Jeevan, & Nilan
-Maria-

"Dad, why do we have to get so many shots?" asked Anjali. "Didn't I just get a shot a few months ago?"

"Yes, you did," said Dad. "But this is a different shot."

"I'm big! I'm six years old. Why do I need another shot?" Anjali asked.

"Even a big, strong six-year-old like you needs shots so you can become a big, healthy seven-year-old," said Dad. "That way you can keep playing soccer and doing all the other things you love."

"I'm scared of getting another shot," Anjali said with a look of concern. "Sometimes they hurt. I'm going to cover my eyes when I get it!"

"You were so brave last time," said Dad. "I'll hold your hand. It will be okay."

"Dad, what's inside the shot?" Anjali asked. "Why do they need to put it in our bodies?"

"These are good questions," Dad replied. "What do you think, should we ask Dr. Amber?"

"Yes, we should ask Dr. Amber," answered Anjali. "I really want to know more about these shots."

"Hi, Anjali. It's nice to see you today," Dr. Amber smiled.

"Anjali is scared of getting a shot today," Dad told Dr. Amber.

"Is that so?" asked Dr. Amber.

"I am," Anjali replied. "Why do we get so many shots? They hurt."

"That's a good question," said Dr. Amber. "I'll tell you why."

"You've had shots since the day you were born," Dr. Amber explained. "They keep you safe from germs. Germs are bad and can cause infections. An *infection* is when these germs get into your body and make you feel really sick."

Dr. Amber continued to explain, "Vaccines are shots that stop you from getting an infection. The vaccine gives your body a small piece of the germ that cannot make you sick. Instead, this small piece of germ helps your body build immunity. *Immunity* is when your body is able to protect you from the bad germs that can make you sick if they enter your body."

How exactly does immunity work?

Your body is made up of building blocks called cells. The body's immune system, which works to build immunity, is made up of special cells that act like superheroes. These superhero cells are found all over your body and keep your body safe.

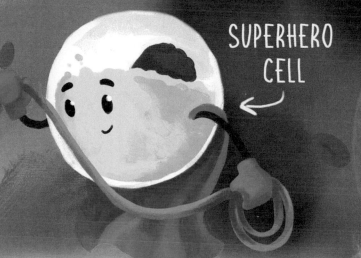

SUPERHERO CELL

ANTIBODY

GERM

Germ pieces from the vaccine can't make you sick. Instead, the vaccine's germ pieces help superhero cells by showing them a picture of what bad germs look like. Then the superhero cells tell their sidekicks, called *antibodies*, to be ready to catch the bad germs before they can make you sick. If superhero cells and their sidekick antibodies ever see the bad germs in your body, they remember what they look like and are ready to protect you.

"So, shots are vaccines that help my body to protect me?" asked Anjali. "And I won't get very sick from the bad germs later?"

"That's right. Once you get the shot, you are **vaccinated**," said Dr. Amber.

"Who figured out how to make vaccines?" Anjali asked.

"The idea behind vaccines began over a thousand years ago. It started in different ways in many parts of the world, including China, India, Iran, Turkey, and Ghana," said Dr. Amber.

"In 1796, the first modern vaccine was created for smallpox by Edward Jenner in England. Smallpox was a disease that caused people to have a lot of painful spots. It was not fun at all to be sick with smallpox!"

"Wow! That was a long time ago!" said Anjali. "Dad, did you get vaccines as a kid too?"

"Oh, yes! I got vaccines too," Dad replied.

"When did kids start getting vaccines?" asked Anjali.

"In 1855, Massachusetts passed a law that all kids had to get the smallpox vaccine before they went to school," explained Dr. Amber. "If each kid got the vaccine, then they would not get sick when they played with each other. Now kids get most of their vaccines before starting first grade, like you did."

"People got the smallpox vaccine for nearly 200 years, so fewer people got sick. In fact, by 1980 there was no more smallpox! We don't need to get the vaccine for smallpox anymore because it went away forever. Isn't that great?"

"It is! I'm happy I need one less shot," said Anjali.

"There are other diseases like polio and chickenpox that used to make older people like your parents and grandparents sick when they were kids," said Dr. Amber. "Most kids don't get these diseases anymore because they got the vaccine."

"What is polio?" asked Anjali.

"When kids had polio, they usually had a fever and a tummy ache," explained Dr. Amber. "For some kids, their legs became so weak that it was hard for them to walk."

"Oh no!" screamed Anjali. "Can that happen to me?"

"Not anymore," Dr. Amber reassured Anjali. "Starting in 1955, kids could get a vaccine, made by the American scientist Jonas Salk, to protect them from polio. Everyone was so eager for the vaccine that they would wait in lines at school to get it."

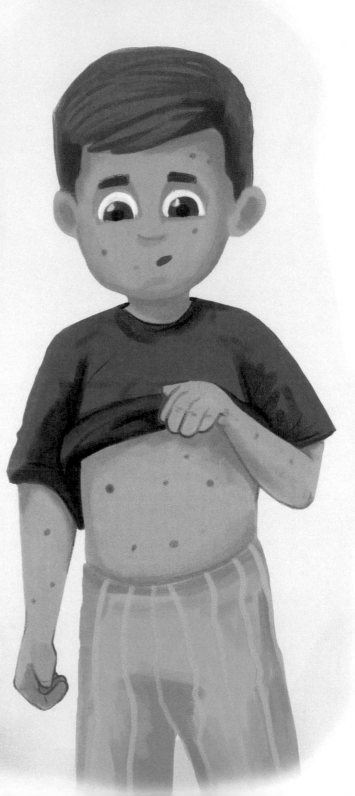

"Do you know what chickenpox is?" asked Dr. Amber.

"I've heard about chickenpox. What is it exactly?" Anjali asked.

"I can tell you about chickenpox," Dad said. "I had it when I was little. It causes you to get spots all over your body, but mostly on your face, belly, and back. I still have a scar on my cheek from chickenpox."

"Will I get it too?" asked Anjali, frightened.

"No. You don't have to worry about getting spots all over because you already got the chickenpox vaccine last year," said Dr. Amber. "That vaccine was developed in the 1970s by Michiaki Takahashi from Japan. Isn't it amazing that you are protected from all of those germs by the vaccines you already got?"

"It is!" Anjali exclaimed.

"But now there is a new germ called COVID-19. It can make you sick, and sometimes it can even make it hard for you to breathe. We wear masks so we don't get sick from COVID-19," Dr. Amber explained.

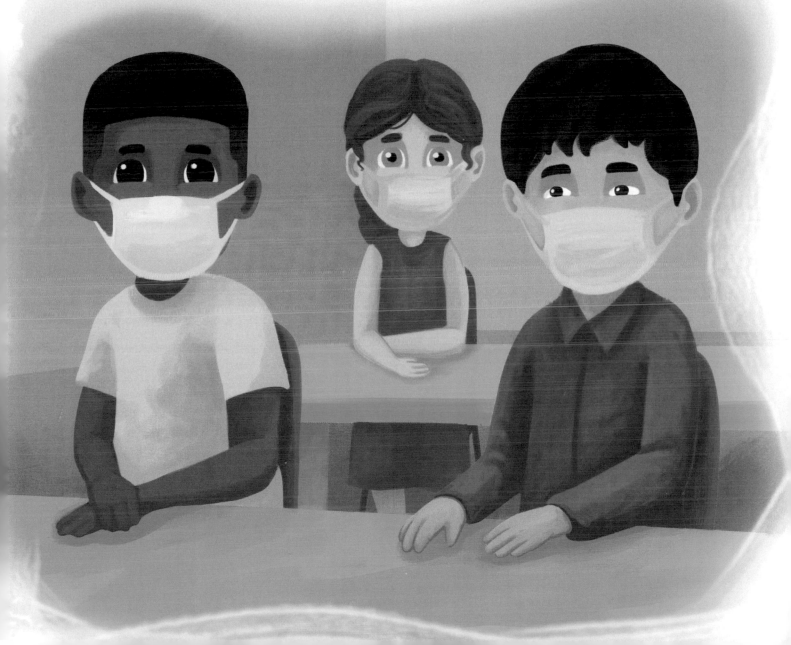

"I don't mind wearing a mask like I do at school, but I don't want to wear one forever," said Anjali.

"Once you receive the vaccine, you will be protected from COVID-19, and you won't have to wear your mask all the time," said Dr. Amber. "People like Hungarian scientist Katalin Karikó helped create the vaccine you will get today."

"Wow! I want to become a scientist too, so I can help people stay healthy," Anjali exclaimed.

"But when can we stop getting shots?" asked Anjali.

"You will always need vaccines, but you need fewer of them as you get older. You'll still get shots when you're a teenager and when you're an adult," said Dr. Amber.

"Some germs are sneaky and can change what they look like. Or sometimes the body forgets what the bad germ looked like. That's why you must get another shot, called a booster shot. A **booster** shot reminds your body what the bad germ looks like so your body can protect you from the bad germ again."

"Remember that smallpox went away when everyone got vaccinated? The germ didn't stay around because almost everyone's body was protected. This is called **herd immunity**. That's why it's important we all get our shots. That's how we can beat COVID-19 and other bad germs!"

"Dr. Amber and I already received the COVID-19 vaccine, and you will get yours today," said Dad.

"I'm glad I can get the vaccine now. Will anything happen after I get it?" Anjali asked.

"Sometimes a vaccine may make you feel a bit crummy. Your arm may hurt, or you may feel tired. But that's just your body building immunity to protect you from the bad germs. If this happens, you will feel better in a day or so," explained Dr. Amber.

"Since you both already got the vaccine, I feel better about getting mine," said Anjali. "I'm ready for it now! Even though I'm scared, I'm going to be brave. Getting a shot keeps me, and everyone I care about, safe."

"Here we go," said Dr. Amber.

Anjali rolled up her sleeve, and
Dr. Amber gave her the shot. It
only took a second!

"That's it!" said Dr. Amber.

"Thank you, Dr. Amber!"
Anjali said. "I'm happy I got
the vaccine. When all my
friends are vaccinated, we
can play together again like
we used to."

"You did great!" said Dr. Amber. "You are so brave, Anjali! I'll see you at your next appointment."

For information about children's vaccines, visit:
https://www.cdc.gov/vaccines/parents/index.html

About the Authors

Dr. Adjoa Smalls-Mantey, MD, DPhil, is a physician-scientist and writer. She conducted viral immunology research for many years, and currently practices psychiatry in New York City. Her mission as a writer is to empower people by sharing information about health, wellness, and mental illness. Dr. Smalls-Mantey loves art and enjoys traveling.

Dr. Maria Abraham, MD, MPH, is a public health physician who has spent her career working in Asia and the United States. She is passionate about improving health outcomes for vulnerable populations. Dr. Abraham is a mother to two boys who keep her busy and always entertained. She and her family enjoy traveling the globe and eating their way through the wonderful neighborhoods of New York City.

Made in the USA
Coppell, TX
09 June 2022

78634007R00024